World Record Underpants

Story by Claire Saxby

Illustrations by Scott Brown

World Record Underpants

Text: Claire Saxby
Publishers: Tania Mazzeo and Eliza Webb
Series consultant: Amanda Sutera
  Hands on Heads Consulting
Editor: Kirsty Hine
Project editor: Annabel Smith
Designer: Jess Kelly
Project designer: Danielle Maccarone
Illustrations: Scott Brown
Production controller: Renee Tome

NovaStar

ISBN 978 0 17 033432 7

Cengage Learning Australia
Level 5, 80 Dorcas Street
Southbank VIC 3006 Australia
Phone: 1300 790 853
Email: aust.nelsonprimary@cengage.com

For learning solutions, visit **cengage.com.au**

Printed in China by 1010 Printing International Ltd
1 2 3 4 5 6 7 28 27 26 25 24

Nelson acknowledges the Traditional Owners and Custodians
of the lands of all First Nations Peoples. We pay respect
to Elders past and present, and extend that respect to
all First Nations Peoples today.

Contents

Chapter 1

The Challenge

"Hey! Look at this!" Miki stopped in front of the school noticeboard. "A world record-setting challenge," he read. "Here. In the hall. On Friday."

"So?" said Han. "It's Tuesday. That's ages away."

"Han, this could make me the most famous kid at our school! In our town!"

"Famous for what?" asked Han.

"For setting a new world record, of course."

Their teacher, Mr Ellis, stopped on his way to the classroom. "Any ideas for what kind of record you might try to set?" he asked.

"Not sure," replied Miki.

"Have fun choosing one," said Mr Ellis, as he walked on.

Han threw a ball high in the air and caught it. "What world record do you want to try to set?"

"Dunno yet," said Miki. "You can have a go, too. Or we can do it together." Miki watched Han bounce his ball again. "Maybe we could bounce that ball or something."

Han shook his head. "No way. I'm not doing anything in front of an audience. Not even in our school hall. I was in a play once, in kindergarten. I was a sheep and a sheepdog bit me."

"A sheepdog bit you? In a kinder play?"
Miki asked.

"Well, a kid dressed as a sheepdog.
And the teacher kept telling me to smile.
Smile! With teeth marks in my leg.
Never again."

"But it'll be fun! Setting a new world
record. C'mon. Please?" Miki pleaded.

"I can help you. I'll be your manager."
Han bounced the ball to Miki, who
bounced it back.

Later that day, after school at Miki's
house, Han filled his mouth with grapes.
Miki's dad finished work early, so Han
went to Miki's after school every day until
his mum picked him up.

"I wonder how many grapes I would
have to put in my mouth for a record?"
asked Miki. "Dad, can we please use the
laptop to look up some world records?"

Dad nodded. "Not too long though.
Then head outside – that trampoline
won't bounce itself!"

There was a record for being the tallest person (2.72 metres). There was a record for having the most babies (69). There was even a record for having the longest fingernails (13 metres).

"I reckon I could grow my nails that long," said Miki. "But maybe not by Friday."

They kept reading.

There was a record for twirling the most hula hoops (200) and for eating the most marshmallows in one minute (21).

Miki peeled a banana. "What about bananas?"

Miki turned to Han. "I love bananas. I could set a record for eating them." As if to prove it, he filled his cheeks with banana and peeled another. It was super-ripe and squishy, so he kept filling his mouth.

"The poster said nothing messy, remember?" Han clicked through to another page.

"Aw," said Miki. "I'm good at messy things. But let's keep looking."

Chapter 2

Which Record?

"Why didn't we think of this yesterday?"
Miki wanted to know. "This record is
going to be easy!"

Miki and Han were at Miki's house the
next day after school, trying new records.

Miki closed his eyes and tipped his
head back.

"Tip your head back more," said Han.
"And you need to go higher, to go further."

Miki opened his eyes and looked at
his friend.

"What does THAT mean?"

"It'll go further. Trust me! I read it on
a website last night."

Miki took a deep breath, closed his
eyes and spat. A watermelon seed shot
out of his mouth. He opened his eyes and
watched it sail through the air.

Miki grinned as Han rolled out the tape measure. "9.36 – no – 9.37 metres. See, I told you it would go further."

"Yeah. But it's still nowhere near far enough," said Miki. He sat on the grass in the backyard and looked at the plate of watermelon seeds.

Dad was picking some lemons nearby. "Didn't the poster say no food?"

"It's a seed!" Miki replied.

"Maybe try something else," said Dad. "Keep looking in that record book you got from the library."

"What about a trampolining record?"
Miki suggested. "Watch this." Miki climbed
onto the trampoline and did a forwards
somersault. Then he did a backwards
somersault.

Han watched.

Miki bounced into a sitting position.
Then he twisted in the air and sat facing
the opposite way. And again. And again.

"I can do this forever," Miki said. He landed on his back, flipped to his front, then to his back again.

"You look like a pancake flipping in a pan," said Han. He flicked through more pages of the record book. "There are some trampolining records here."

Miki jumped off the trampoline and grabbed the book.

"What's the record?" he asked. "Can I do it?"

Han grabbed the book back.

"Not unless you can beat a ... 'septuple twisting backwards somersault'. Or something like that," said Han.

Miki thought that septuple meant seven. He hoped it didn't.

"Yup," said Han. "Seven."

Miki flopped down on the grass, covering his face with his hands.

"This is too hard. It's already Wednesday. We'll never be ready to set a new record by Friday."

Chapter 3

An Unusual Idea

At school on Thursday, all anyone could talk about was the record-setting challenge. It was going to be so much fun. If only Miki and Han could decide on what Miki would do.

Miki wanted to do something wild, like clip pegs to Han's face (52 was the current record). Han reminded Miki that he wasn't doing anything in front of an audience and that pegs would hurt.

"But we're running out of time. I'm going to miss out on my one chance to be famous," said Miki.

At lunchtime, Miki and Han watched as everyone practised. A group of boys were trying to pack their school bags in record time. Some girls were throwing soft toys into a bucket. Their friend Amina was flipping a full water bottle.

Han nudged Miki. "Look! Why didn't we think of that?" A girl was balancing a ball on her head, while her friend timed her.

"We have until the end of lunch to decide what we're doing and enter the challenge," said Miki. "Let's go to the library and have another look on the world records website."

They found hundreds of records on the internet, but nothing was right.

Miki tried holding his breath. It was nowhere near a record time. He poked out his tongue and Han measured the length. Nup. Way too short for a record.

"Maybe I could stay still for 37 hours."

Han looked at him.

"Right. I'm not so good at staying still."
Miki's shoulders slouched in defeat.
"I never thought setting a world record would be so hard."

"Me neither," said Han. "Pity you can't walk on your hands."

"Or juggle," added Miki.

"Or snore."

"Or sneeze a lot."

Miki was ready to give up.

Then Han exclaimed, "Getting dressed! That's it!" He pointed at the screen where a teenager stood, arms stretched wide. She was wearing a lot of T-shirts layered on top of each other. "Whoa, that's a lot to put on in just one minute!"

Miki stomped around the library, pretending he was wearing all those clothes. "I can do that! We can practise tonight. Quick, let's go and write our details on the sign-up sheet."

"Sorry, Miki. We already have a team signed-up for T-shirt layers," said Mr Ellis, who was standing near the sign-up sheet when the boys got there. "Do you have another idea?"

The three-minutes-before-end-of-lunch music started. Miki couldn't believe it. They finally found a record they had a good chance of beating and they were too late! If they didn't think of something now, they were going to miss out.

"Underwear," hissed Han. "Just write 'underwear layers'."

Miki frowned. "You've got to be joking!"

Han shook his head. "Nah, it's perfect. Even better than T-shirts. All you have to do is put on lots of pairs of underpants, one on top of the other. In one minute. You can do it. Easy."

Miki stared at Han. "You're too scared to stand in front of an audience, but you want me to show my underpants – ALL of them?"

Han nodded.

"I can't stand naked in front of the whole school."

"You'd have the first pair of underpants on already. Or bike shorts. And your shirt. And socks. Almost completely dressed."

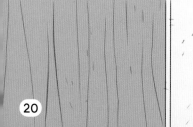

Miki was silent as he thought about putting on layer after layer of underpants. But he knew he could do it. He imagined his victory bow. He was going to be famous! The end-of-lunch bell rang.

"What do you think?" asked Han.

"Yeah, let's do it!"

Chapter 4

Practice Makes Perfect

"I give up!" Mr Ellis put down the novel he was reading to the class after lunch. "I know it's difficult to sit quietly when there are world records to be set. So this afternoon I'm going to let you practise for the challenge – using maths! Think about how maths will help you break your record."

Miki looked at Han, puzzled. "How is maths connected to underpants?" he asked Han.

Han juggled his pencil from hand to hand. "The world record is seventeen pairs of underpants in one minute, so you have to be faster than that to get eighteen pairs on in the same time. Or less."

Sixty seconds. Eighteen pairs. The boys were quiet as they worked it out. Miki would have to put on a pair of underpants every three seconds. That left a few extra seconds in case he slowed down or made a mistake.

"I can do eighteen," said Miki, after the boys had finished calculating. "I can do it easily!"

At Miki's place after school, the boys dropped their bags by the front door and headed to Miki's bedroom.

Miki opened his underwear drawer and pulled out all of his underpants. There were nowhere near enough for a world record. They checked the clothesline and the washing basket and found more, but they were still several pairs short.

"Don't you put your old pairs in a rag bag?" asked Han.

Miki shook his head.

"You could use your dad's underpants?"
Then Han grinned. "Or my gran's!"

"There is no way I'm wearing nanna knickers! No. Way."

While they thought about where to get more pairs, they tested out how to set up the underpants for the challenge. They tried laying them side-by-side across the back porch and then one in front of the other.

"It's a lot easier jumping forward," said Miki.

By the time Dad called them for an afternoon snack, Miki was jumping into each pair and dragging them up over his legs without falling over.

"You look like a frog," said Han.
He paused as they sat at the table.
Han grinned. "You could use my gran's undies. It might be good to have some bigger ones at the end."

"Ew. Thanks, but no."

"I have a brand-new pack," said Dad.

Miki and Han exchanged glances before Miki nodded.

Miki kept practising after Han went home. He kept going until bedtime.

That night, he dreamed of frogs and underpants – and frogs wearing underpants.

When the sun pushed through the gap in his curtains, Miki leapt out of bed.
It was Friday, and today he and Han were going to set a new world record!

Chapter 5

The Big Day

"Line up at the door please," said Mr Ellis on Friday morning. The students made their way to the hall as he told everyone the rules again.

Finally, it was time.

The lid came off Amina's bottle as she flipped it a fourth time, and she was disqualified.

Two girls landed their eleventh soft toy in a bucket just as the 30-second timer buzzed. A new record!

Miki and Han were last. By then, seven new records had been set. They arranged the underpants from the back of the stage to the front, with Dad's new ones last.

Mr Ellis watched as Han got ready with the timer. Then Han yelled, "Go!"

Jump, pull up. Jump, pull up. Miki focused on jumping and pulling up in one smooth action.

"Thirty seconds left!" called Han.

Miki kept going. Jump, pull up. Jump, pull up.

The whole school was counting down with Han. "Four, three, two, one! Stop!"

Miki's heart sank. He still had one pair left to go.

Han was dancing in circles. "We did it! We did it!"

"But there's one pair left," said Miki.

Han grinned. "I put out an extra pair."

"So we beat the old record?" asked Miki.

Han nodded.

The class clapped and whooped.

"Woo hoo!" Han threw his arms around Miki and lifted him up into the air. "We set a new world record!"

It wasn't until later that day that Miki remembered something.

"Han? Where did the extra pair of underpants come from?"

Han pulled his ball from his pocket and started bouncing. "Setting a new record was so much fun! Maybe next time there's a challenge I can set the record and you can be my manager."

"Han?"

"Oh, the extra underpants?" He grinned. "From our rag bag. They might have been my gran's!"

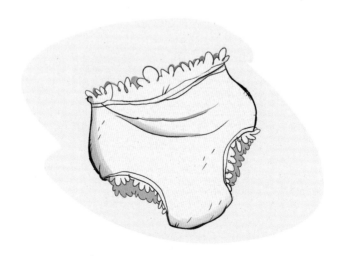